First
Facts®

U.S. Military Forces

# THE UNITED STATES AIR FORCE

BY MICHAEL GREEN

CAPSTONE PRESS
a capstone imprint

First Facts are published by Capstone Press,
1710 Roe Crest Drive, North Mankato, Minnesota 56003
www.capstonepub.com

Library of Congress Cataloging-in-Publication Data

Green, Michael, 1952–
    The United States Air Force / by Michael Green.
    p. cm.—(First facts. U.S. Military Forces.)
    Audience: Grades K-3.
    Summary: "Provides information on the training, missions, and equipment used by the
United States Air Force"—Provided by publisher.
    Includes bibliographical references and index.
    ISBN 978-1-4765-0071-3 (library binding)
    ISBN 978-1-4765-1584-7 (eBook PDF)
1. United States. Air Force—Juvenile literature. I. Title.
UG633.G725 2013
358.400973—dc23                                          2012033246

Editorial Credits

Aaron Sautter, editor; Ashlee Suker, designer; Eric Manske, production specialist


Photo Credits

DoD photo by Airman 1st Class Chad Warren, USAF, 18; Getty Images: Time Life Pictures/J.R. Eyerman, 6;
U.S. Air Force, 21, Airman 1st Class Benjamin Wiseman, 17, Dennis Rogers, 13, Mike Kaplan, 15, Staff Sgt.
Chad Thompson, cover, Staff Sgt. Christopher Hummel, 11, Tech Sgt. Bennie J. Davis III, 10, Tech Sgt. Justin
D. Pyle, 1, Master Sgt. Scott T. Sturkol, 9, Staff Sgt. Michael B. Keller, 5


Artistic Effects

Shutterstock: Kirsty Pargeter, Redshinestudio, Vilmos Varga

Printed in the United States of America in North Mankato, Minnesota.
092012    006933CGS13

# TABLE OF CONTENTS

# CHAPTER ONE

# AIR DEFENSES

U.S. Air Force fighter planes fly over Afghanistan. Suddenly, enemy forces attack U.S. soldiers on the ground. The planes race to help protect the soldiers. They fire **missiles** at the enemy's position, ending the **firefight**. Thanks to the U.S. Air Force, the ground troops are safe.

missile—an explosive weapon that can travel long distances
firefight—an exchange of weapon fire between two military units

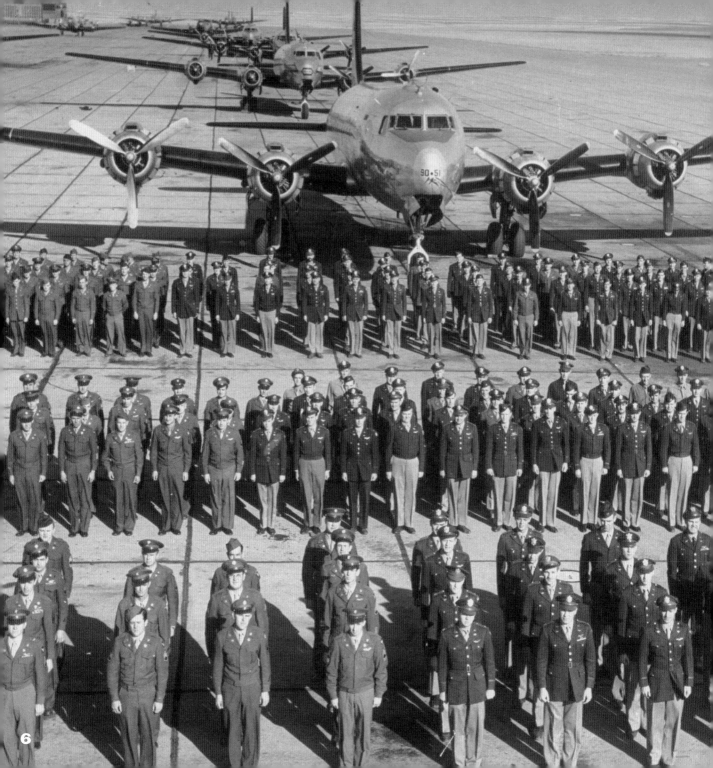

The U.S. Air Force is a powerful part of the U.S. Armed Forces. It defends the United States and helps protect **allies** around the world. The Air Force's planes quickly respond wherever they are needed.

The Air Force began in 1907 as part of the U.S. Army. It became a separate military force on October 14, 1947.

**FACT**
The Air Force often supports search and rescue missions and fights large forest fires.

ally—a person or country that helps and supports another

# CHAPTER TWO

# AWESOME AIR POWER

The U.S. Air Force is the strongest air power in the world. More than 330,000 active **airmen** serve in the Air Force. More than 216,000 people serve in the reserves. The Air Force uses more than 5,000 aircraft. It also controls more than 50 space **satellites**.

**airman**—someone who serves in the Air Force

**satellite**—a spacecraft that circles the earth; satellites gather and send information

## FACT

Men and women in the
U.S. Air Force are
known as "airmen."

Most airmen are **enlisted**. These men and women help keep the Air Force running smoothly every day. Airmen maintain planes, program computers, and work with spacecraft.

Air Force officers lead airmen. They make important decisions during **missions** and give orders. Pilots, combat specialists, and missile commanders are all Air Force officers.

enlist—to voluntarily join a branch of the military

mission—a military task

# CHAPTER THREE

# BECOMING AN AIRMAN

Air Force **recruits** go through eight weeks of basic training. They do push-ups, sit-ups, and run through **obstacle courses**. They also learn survival skills and how to use weapons.

After basic training, airmen go to technical school. They learn skills needed for their Air Force jobs. Some airmen are engineers or doctors. Others work with computers, space systems, and many other jobs.

**recruit**—a new member of the armed forces

**obstacle course**—a series of barriers that airmen must jump over, climb, or crawl through

Some people become Air Force officers at the Air Force Academy in Colorado. **Cadets** learn leadership skills while earning a college degree. They then serve at least eight years as an officer.

People who have a college degree can go to Officer Training School. There they learn battle and leadership skills. They become Air Force officers when they graduate.

**cadet**—a military student

**FACT**

College students can join the Air Force Reserve Officer Training Corps (AFROTC). They take college classes to learn skills needed to become an officer.

# CHAPTER FOUR

# FLYING INTO BATTLE

The U.S. Air Force has more planes than any military force in the world. Fighter planes such as the A-10 Thunderbolt carry powerful missiles and machine guns. The B-52 Stratofortress and other bombers drop bombs on enemy positions.

## FACT

The Air Force also uses unmanned planes. The MQ-1 Predator and MQ-9 Reaper are used to fight enemies from hundreds of miles away.

A-10 THUNDERBOLTS

E-3 SENTRY

USAF

## FACT
The U.S. Air Force uses nearly 100 different kinds of aircraft.

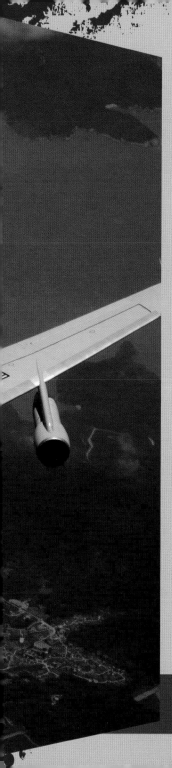

The Air Force uses many other aircraft. The U-2 Dragon Lady and other spy planes help find hidden enemy locations. The E-3 Sentry uses advanced **radar** to find and fight enemies. Helicopters such as the UH-1 Iroquois carry troops and gear to places planes can't reach.

**radar**—a device that uses radio waves to track the location of objects

# CHAPTER FIVE

# DEFENDING THE SKIES

Air Force Space Command (AFSC) works from space to defend the United States. It uses satellites to guide missions in other countries. Satellites also watch for enemy missile attacks.

The world's best pilots, airmen, and aircraft serve in the U.S. Air Force. They protect America and keep the skies safe.

# GLOSSARY

**airman** (AYR-man)—someone who serves in the Air Force

**ally** (AL-eye)—a person or country that helps and supports another

**cadet** (kuh-DET)—a military student

**enlist** (en-LIST)—to voluntarily join a branch of the military

**firefight** (FIRE-fite)—an exchange of weapon fire between two military units

**missile** (MISS-uhl)—an explosive weapon that can travel long distances

**mission** (MISH-uhn)—a military task

**obstacle course** (OB-stuh-kuhl KORSS)—a series of barriers that airmen must jump over, climb, or crawl through

**radar** (RAY-dar)—a device that uses radio waves to track the location of objects

**recruit** (ri-KROOT)—a new member of the armed forces

**satellite** (SAT-uh-lite)—a spacecraft that circles the earth; satellites gather and send information

# READ MORE

**Goldish, Meish.** *Air Force: Civilian to Airman.* Becoming a Soldier. New York: Bearport Pub., 2011.

**Loria, Laura.** *Air Force.* New York: Gareth Stevens Pub., 2011.

**Zobel, Derek.** *United States Air Force.* Armed Forces. Minneapolis: Bellwether Media, 2008.

# INTERNET SITES

FactHound offers a safe, fun way to find Internet sites related to this book. All of the sites on FactHound have been researched by our staff.

Here's all you do:

Visit *www.facthound.com*

Type in this code: 9781476500713

**Super-cool stuff!** Check out projects, games and lots more at **www.capstonekids.com**

# INDEX